Octopuses

James Maclaine

Illustrated by Wazza Pink
Additional illustrations by Gal Weizman

Designed by Gabriel Liu, Helena Towell and Sam Whibley

Octopus consultant: Professor Steve Simpson,
Marine Biology and Global Change, University of Bristol

Contents

Where do they live?

Octopuses live in seas and oceans around the world.

This day octopus is swimming in the Pacific Ocean, near Hawaii.

There are about 300 different kinds of octopuses.

All arms

Every octopus has eight long arms.

The round, cup-shaped parts along each arm are called suckers.

Sucker

Octopuses use their arms and suckers to crawl in any direction.

This octopus clings to the sea floor with its suckers.

Then it stretches or scrunches its arms...

...to push and pull itself along.

Jet-powered swimmers

If an octopus needs to move quickly, it can swim.

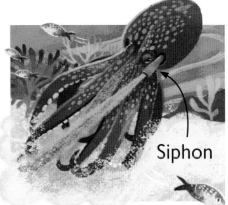

Siphon

First, the octopus sucks in water so its body swells up.

Then it squirts the water out of a tube called a siphon.

This jet of water shoots the octopus a short distance. Its arms trail behind.

An octopus can point its siphon to swim in a different direction.

This Atlantic white-spotted octopus is diving down.

Umbrella octopuses just drift through the ocean. They open their arms wide.

A tight squeeze

Octopuses have soft, squishy bodies, so they can fit into surprisingly narrow gaps.

An octopus feels its way to a crack in the sea floor.

The octopus slips its arms inside, one by one.

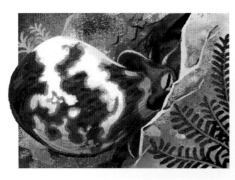

Then it squeezes the rest of its body into the crack too.

The octopus hides inside. This place is called its den.

Giant Pacific octopuses sometimes sneak through holes in fishing nets to steal crabs.

This octopus has found a small jar at the bottom of the sea to use for its den.

Hunting for food

Octopuses eat all kinds of sea creatures.
They catch them with their arms.

This octopus is hunting on a reef.
It's stretching the skin between
its arms to make a trap.

Algae octopuses hunt in pools of water near the seashore.

If an algae octopus can't find anything to eat, it climbs out.

The octopus moves over rocks to reach another pool.

Then it slips into the water to search for food there.

Time to eat

Octopuses have tough beaks under their bodies that they use to eat.

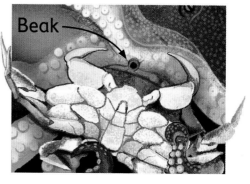

Beak

An octopus drags a crab to its den before it starts to eat.

Inside the den, the octopus pulls the crab to its beak.

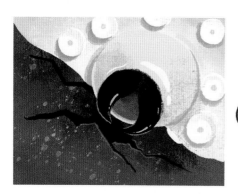

Then it bites through the crab's shell to make a hole.

The octopus eats the soft parts. It doesn't eat the shell.

This octopus is tossing out some clam shells.
Octopuses tidy their dens after eating.

Octopus eggs

Female octopuses lay eggs. They usually stick them to rocks.

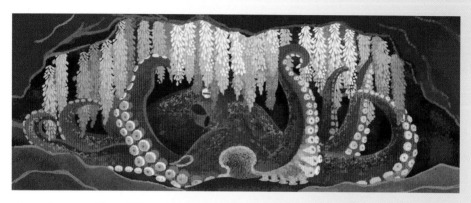

A giant Pacific octopus hangs thousands of eggs from the rocky roof of her den.

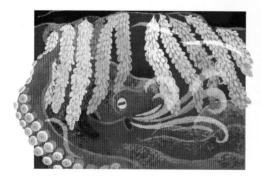

For many months, she blows clean water over the eggs to keep them alive.

Inside each egg, a baby octopus grows until it's big enough to hatch.

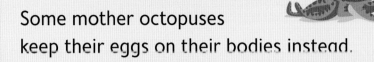

Some mother octopuses
keep their eggs on their bodies instead.

This female argonaut octopus carries
her eggs. She grows a shell-like case
to protect them.

Case

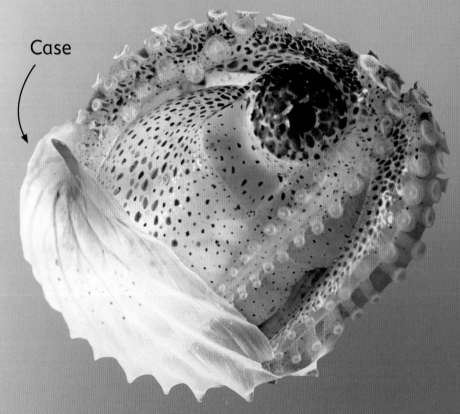

Baby octopuses

When they hatch, baby octopuses are no bigger than a pea. They grow up quickly.

This baby octopus has just left its egg.

After hatching, most baby octopuses drift through the sea.

They try to catch tiny creatures called zooplankton to eat.

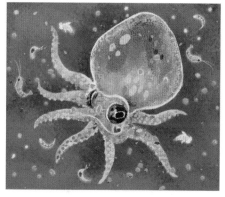

As an octopus gets bigger, it sinks to the sea floor.

Baby octopuses often turn brighter or darker and then change back again.

Blending in

Octopuses can change the way they look to hide from sea creatures that eat them.

A Maori octopus spots a dangerous sea lion and swims to some seaweed.

As soon as it lands on the weed, its skin turns bright red to match.

The octopus's skin also gets bumpier so it looks as frilly as the weed.

This veiled octopus is blending in
with the reef where it lives.

Masters of disguise

Mimic octopuses scare off hunters by pretending to be poisonous animals.

The arms of a mimic octopus are very thin.

The octopus clumps its arms together...

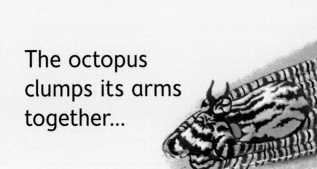

...to make the shape of this poisonous fish.

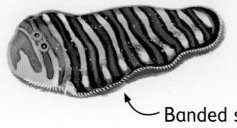

Banded sole

It buries six arms in the sand and wiggles just two...

...to look like this poisonous snake.

Sea krait

Octopus tools

Some octopuses are so clever that they can learn how to use tools.

This veined octopus is carrying half a coconut shell for a hiding place.

Octopuses sometimes cover their bodies with lots of seashells.

Tiny male blanket octopuses use tentacles that sting. They steal them from creatures called bluebottles.

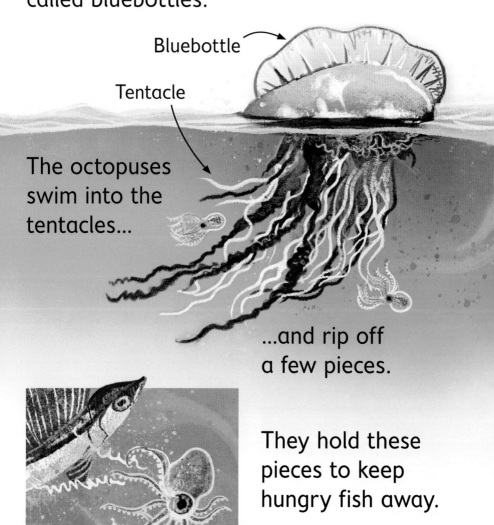

Bluebottle

Tentacle

The octopuses swim into the tentacles...

...and rip off a few pieces.

They hold these pieces to keep hungry fish away.

Octopus against octopus

Octopuses live alone. If they get too close to each other, they might fight.

A gloomy octopus sprays sand at another octopus to tell it to go away.

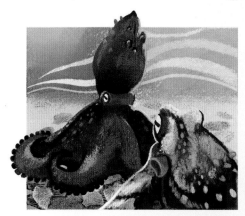

It also makes itself look tall and turns its skin dark.

Sometimes, it swims at the other octopus to chase it off.

These octopuses
are wrestling over
the best shells
to hide in.

The winner keeps the other octopus's shells.

Keep back!

Octopuses have surprising ways to startle animals that try to attack them.

Bright blue rings flash over this little octopus's body.

The rings tell other creatures to stay away.

Most octopuses make a black liquid called ink.

An octopus shoots its ink at an eel that tries to bite it.

The eel can't see through the ink, so the octopus has time to escape.

Down in the deep

Amazing types of octopuses live deep down in the ocean where no sunlight can reach.

This glowing sucker octopus has two fins on its body.

Fins

It flaps its fins up and down to move through the water.

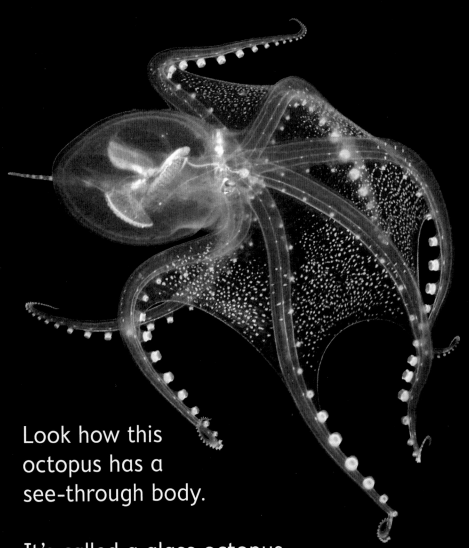

Look how this
octopus has a
see-through body.

It's called a glass octopus.

Some deep-sea octopuses are
found near hot water that spurts
from the sea floor.

Glossary

Here are some of the words in this book you might not know. This page tells you what they mean.

 sucker - a round part on an octopus's arm that clings by sucking.

 siphon - a tube-shaped part. Octopuses squirt water from their siphons.

 den - the place where an animal rests, sleeps or hides.

 beak - two hard, sharp mouth parts. Octopuses bite with their beaks.

 tentacle - a long, thin body part. Some sea creatures have tentacles that sting.

 ink - a dark liquid. Octopuses shoot ink to confuse other animals.

 fin - a flat body part. Fish, dolphins, whales and some octopuses have fins.

Usborne Quicklinks

Would you like to find out more about octopuses, see where they live, and watch how they move? Visit Usborne Quicklinks for links to websites with videos, facts and activities.

 Scan the code or go to **usborne.com/Quicklinks** and type in the keywords "**beginners octopuses**". Make sure you ask a grown-up before going online.

Notes for grown-ups

Please read the internet safety guidelines at Usborne Quicklinks with your child. Children should be supervised online. The websites are regularly reviewed and the links at Usborne Quicklinks are updated. Usborne Publishing is not responsible for the content or availability of external websites.

This long-armed octopus is peeping out from its den.

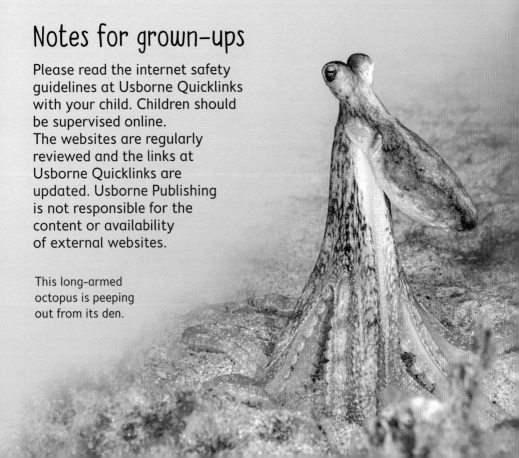

Index

Acknowledgements

Photographic manipulation by John Russell and Nick Wakeford

Photo credits

The publishers are grateful to the following for permission to reproduce material:
cover © Blue Planet Archive / Andy Murch; **p.1** © MadeleinWolf / Alamy Stock Photo;
pp.2-3 © David Fleetham / naturepl.com; **p.4** © Andy Murch / naturepl.com; **p.7** © Sergio Hanquet / naturepl.com;
pp.8-9 © Blue Planet Archive / Alamy Stock Photo; **p.10** © Marli Wakeling / Alamy Stock Photo;
p.13 © Blue Planet Archive / Anestis Rekkas; **p.15** © David Shale / naturepl.com;
p.16 © Blue Planet Archive / John C. Lewis; **p.19** © Blue Planet Archive / Martin Strmiska; **p.20** © Michael Aw;
p.22 © Mike Veitch / Alamy Stock Photo; **p.25** © Steve Jones / Stocktrek Images, Inc. / Alamy Stock Photo;
p.26 © SeaTops / Alamy Stock Photo; **p.28** © David Shale / naturepl.com;
p.29 © Schmidt Ocean Institute; **p.31** © Blue Planet Archive / Doug Perrine.

Every effort has been made to trace and acknowledge ownership of copyright. If any rights have
been omitted, the publishers offer to rectify this in any subsequent editions following notification.

Sun, Moon and Stars

Farm Animals

Elizabeth I

Rubbish & Recycling

Dogs

Horses & Ponies

Cats

Ancient Greeks

Spiders

VOLCANOES

DINOSAURS

Your Body

Armour

Sharks

The Celts

VIKINGS

Castles

How flowers grow

Digging up the past

Caterpillars & Butterflies

Ballet

Pirates

EGYPTIANS

Eggs & Chicks

ROMANS

Weather

Tadpoles & Frogs

Why do we eat?

Under the Sea

Bears

AZTECS

Usborne Beginners
Trucks

Usborne Beginners
Night Animals

Usborne Beginners
Firefighters

Usborne Beginners
Antarctica

Usborne Beginners
Bugs

COWBOYS

Usborne Beginners
PLANET EARTH

Usborne Beginners
London

Usborne Beginners
Seashore

Usborne Beginners
China

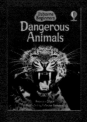
Usborne Beginners
Dangerous Animals

Usborne Beginners
Rainforests

Usborne Beginners
Trees

Usborne Beginners
Bats

Ships

Usborne Beginners
Reptiles

Usborne Beginners
Trains

Usborne Beginners
Knights

Usborne Beginners
The Solar System

Monkeys

Usborne Beginners
Penguins

Usborne Beginners
Elephants

Usborne Beginners
Tigers

Usborne Beginners
Earthquakes & Tsunamis

Usborne Beginners
Storms and Hurricanes

Usborne Beginners
BEES & WASPS

Usborne Beginners
Wolves

Usborne Beginners
Owls

Usborne Beginners
Snakes